BOTANICAL SANCTUARIES

Arkansas Ecoregions

- Ozark Highlands
- Boston Mountains
- Arkansas Valley
- Ouachita Mountains
- Mississippi Valley Loess Plains
- Mississippi Alluvial Plain
- South Central Plains

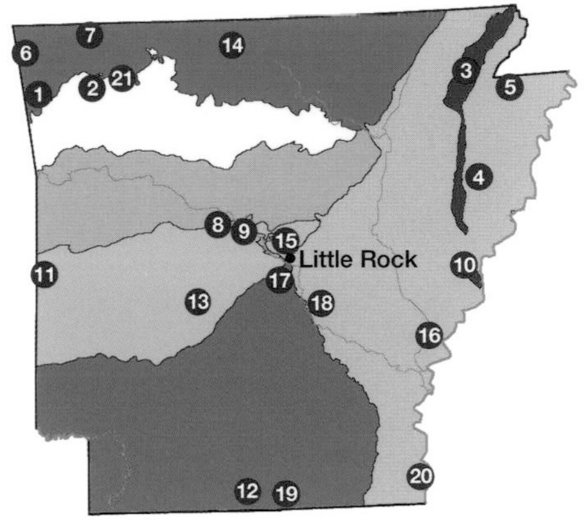

1. Devil's Den State Park
2. Botanical Garden of the Ozarks
3. Lake Charles State Park
4. Crowley's Ridge/ Village Creek State Park
5. Big Lake National Wildlife Refuge
6. Ozark National Forest
7. Blue Springs Heritage Center
8. Mount Nebo State Park
9. Petit Jean State Park
10. St. Francis National Forest
11. Queen Wilhelmina State Park
12. South Arkansas Arboretum
13. Garvan Woodland Gardens
14. Bull Shoals White River State Park
15. Historic Arkansas Museum
16. White River National Wildlife Refuge
17. Arkansas Arboretum (Pinnacle Mt. State Park)
18. Delta Rivers Nature Center
19. Felsenthal National Wildlife Refuge
20. Lake Chicot State Park
21. Hobbs State Park Conservation Area

Measurements denote the height of plants unless otherwise indicated. Illustrations are not to scale.

N.B. – Many edible wild plants have poisonous mimics. Never eat a wild plant or fruit unless you are absolutely sure it is safe to do so. The publisher makes no representation or warranties with respect to the accuracy, completeness, correctness or usefulness of this information and specifically disclaims any implied warranties of fitness for a particular purpose. The advice, strategies and/or techniques contained herein may not be suitable for all individuals. The publisher shall not be responsible for any physical harm (up to and including death), loss of profit or other commercial damage. The publisher assumes no liability brought or instituted by individuals or organizations arising out of or relating in any way to the application and/or use of the information, advice and strategies contained herein.

Made in the USA

Waterford Press publishes reference guides that introduce readers to nature observation, outdoor recreation and survival skills. Product information is featured on the website: **www.waterfordpress.com**

Text & illustrations © 2008, 2023 Waterford Press Inc. All rights reserved. Photos © Shutterstock. Ecoregion map © The National Atlas of the United States.

To order or for information on custom published products, please call 800-434-2555 or email orderdesk@waterfordpress.com. For permissions or to share comments, email editor@waterfordpress.com.

ISBN 978-1-58355-404-3 $7.95 U.S.

50795

9 781583 554043

UPC 8 84682 00923 6

10 9 8 7 6 5 4 3 2 1 2306807

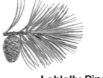

ARKANSAS TREES & WILDFLOWERS – A Folding Pocket Guide to Familiar Plants

WATERFORD PRESS

A POCKET NATURALIST® GUIDE

ARKANSAS TREES & WILDFLOWERS

A Folding Pocket Guide to Familiar Plants

T0123965

TREES & SHRUBS

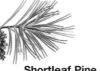

Shortleaf Pine
Pinus echinata To 100 ft. (30 m)
Flexible needles grow in bundles of 2-3. Egg-shaped cones have thin scales ending in a small prickle.

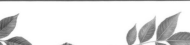

Loblolly Pine
Pinus taeda To 100 ft. (30 m)
Long needles grow in bundles of 3. Oblong cones have scales armed with a curved spine. **Arkansas' state tree.**

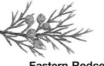

Eastern Redcedar
Juniperus virginiana To 60 ft. (18 m)
4-sided branchlets are covered with overlapping, scale-like leaves. Fruit is a blue berry.

Baldcypress
Taxodium distichum To 120 ft. (36.5 m)
Note flaring trunk. Leaves are flattened and feathery. Protruding root "knees" help to stabilize the tree in wet areas.

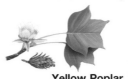

Yellow Poplar (Tuliptree)
Liriodendron tulipifera To 120 ft. (36.5 m)
Note unusual leaf shape. Showy flowers are succeeded by cone-like aggregates of papery, winged seeds.

Red Maple
Acer rubrum To 90 ft. (27 m)
Leaves have 3-5 lobes and turn scarletin autumn. Flowers are succeeded by red, winged seed pairs.

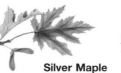

Silver Maple
Acer saccharinum To 80 ft. (24 m)
Note short trunk and spreading crown. 5-lobed leaves are silvery beneath.

Sugar Maple
Acer saccharum To 100 ft. (30 m)
Leaves have five coarsely-toothed lobes. Fruit is a winged seed pair. Tree sap is the source of maple syrup.

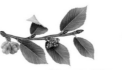

Slippery Elm
Ulmus rubra To 70 ft. (21 m)
Rough leaves are coarsely-toothed. Bark has vertical ridges. Papery fruits have a hairy seed cavity.

American Elm
Ulmus americana To 100 ft. (30 m)
Note vase-shaped profile. Leaves are toothed. Fruits have a papery collar and are notched at the tip.

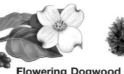

Flowering Dogwood
Cornus florida To 30 ft. (9 m)
Tiny yellow flowers bloom in crowded clusters surrounded by 4 white petal-like structures.

Post Oak
Quercus stellata To 70 ft. (21 m)
Deeply lobed, leathery leaves are cross-shaped.

TREES & SHRUBS

White Oak
Quercus alba To 100 ft. (30 m)
Leaves have 5-9 rounded lobes. Acorn has a shallow, scaly cup.

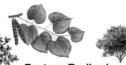

Black Oak
Quercus velutina To 80 ft. (24 m)
Leaves have 5-7 spiny lobes. Acorns have a ragged-edged cup.

Southern Red Oak
Quercus falcata To 80 ft. (24 m)
Leaves have 3-7 deep lobes and are hairy beneath.

Chinkapin Oak
Quercus muehlenbergii To 80 ft. (24 m)
Leaves are up to 6 in. (15 cm) long and are coarsely-toothed.

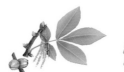

Common Serviceberry
Amelanchier arborea To 40 ft. (12 m)
White, star-shaped flowers bloom early in spring. Red to purple-black berries ripen in mid-summer.

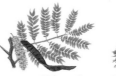

Shagbark Hickory
Carya ovata To 100 ft. (30 m)
Bark curls away from the trunk, giving it a shaggy appearance. Leaves have 5 leaflets.

Mockernut Hickory
Carya tomentosa To 80 ft. (24 m)
Rounded, thick-shelled fruits have 4 prominent grooves. Fruits are sweet.

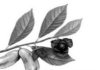

Pawpaw
Asimina triloba To 30 ft. (9 m)
Large leaves, to 12 in. (30 cm) long, turn yellow when fruits ripen. Oblong fruits blacken when ripe.

Northern Catalpa
Catalpa speciosa To 80 ft. (24 m)
Leaves are heart-shaped. Flowers have five fringed lobes. Fruits are bean-like.

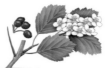

Hawthorn
Crataegus spp. To 40 ft. (12 m)
Tree has rounded crown of spiny branches. Apple-like fruits appear in summer.

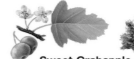

White Fringetree
Chionanthus virginicus To 30 ft. (9 m)
Note short trunk. Fragrant flowers bloom in large showy clusters.

Sweet Crabapple
Malus coronaria To 30 ft. (9 m)
Fragrant white flowers bloom in late spring and are succeeded by small, oblong, yellow-green apples. **The apple blossom is Arkansas' state flower.**

TREES & SHRUBS

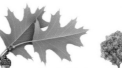

White Ash
Fraxinus americana To 80 ft. (24 m)
Leaves usually have 7 leaflets. Flowers are succeeded by papery samaras.

Green Ash
Fraxinus pennsylvanica To 60 ft. (18 m)
Leaves have 7-9 leaflets. Flowers are succeeded by single-winged fruits.

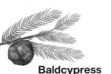

Eastern Redbud
Cercis canadensis To 40 ft. (12 m)
Showy magenta flowers are succeeded by oblong seed pods.

Black Locust
Robinia pseudoacacia To 80 ft. (24 m)
Leaves have 7-19 leaflets. Thorn size up to 2 in. (5 cm). Black seed pods are up to 4 in. (10 cm) long.

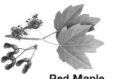

Honey Locust
Gleditsia triacanthos To 80 ft. (24 m)
Leaves have 7-15 pairs of leaflets. Thorn size up to 10 in. (25 cm). Twisted fruits are up to 16 in. (40 cm) long.

Common Persimmon
Diospyros virginiana To 70 ft. (21 m)
Shrub or tree has urn-shaped flowers that are succeeded by round fruits.

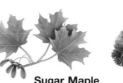

Black Tupelo
Nyssa sylvatica To 100 ft. (30 m)
Glossy leaves turn red in autumn. Blue fruits have ridged seeds.

Sweetgum
Liquidambar styraciflua To 100 ft. (30 m)
Small, greenish flowers bloom in tight, round clusters and are succeeded by hard fruits covered with woody spines.

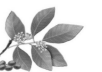

American Sycamore
Platanus occidentalis To 100 ft. (30 m)
Leaves have 3-5 shallow lobes. Rounded fruits are bristly.

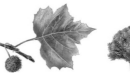

American Basswood
Tilia americana To 100 ft. (30 m)
Leaves are heart-shaped. Flowers and nutlets hang from narrow leafy bracts. Often multi-trunked.

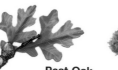

Eastern Cottonwood
Populus deltoides To 100 ft. (30 m)
Leaves are up to 7 in. (18 cm) long. Flowers are succeeded by capsules containing seeds with cottony "tails."

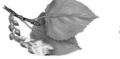

American Plum
Prunus americana To 30 ft. (9 m)
Oval leaves have toothed edges. Bright red fruits have yellow flesh.

TREES & SHRUBS

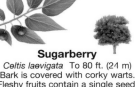

Sassafras
Sassafras albidum To 60 ft. (18 m)
Aromatic tree or shrub has leaves that are mitten-shaped or 3-lobed. Fruits are dark berries.

Sugarberry
Celtis laevigata To 80 ft. (24 m)
Bark is covered with corky warts. Fleshy fruits contain a single seed.

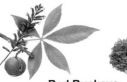

Black Cherry
Prunus serotina To 80 ft. (24 m)
Aromatic bark and leaves smell cherry-like. Dark berries have an oval stone inside.

Red Buckeye
Aesculus pavia To 20 ft. (6 m)
Tree or shrub grows in moist soils. Leaves have 5-7 leaflets. Nut-like fruits contain 1-2 poisonous seeds.

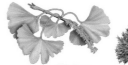

Ginkgo
Ginkgo biloba To 70 ft. (21 m)
Chinese native is often planted in urban areas. Fan-shaped leaves are distinctive.

American Holly
Ilex opaca To 70 ft. (21 m)
Tree or shrub is distinguished by its stiff, spiny evergreen leaves and red, poisonous berries.

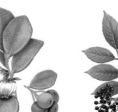

Bog Blueberry
Vaccinium spp.
To 2 ft. (60 cm)
Bell-shaped, pinkish flowers bloom in June and are succeeded by blue berries in summer.

American Elder
Sambucus canadensis
To 16 ft. (4.8 cm)
Shrub or small tree. Saw-toothed leaves have 5-7 leaflets. Flowers are succeeded by dark berries.

Kudzu
Pueraria montana
Vine to 16 ft. (18 m)
Introduced, invasive species often overruns buildings and fencerows.

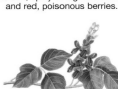

Arrowwood
Viburnum dentatum
To 10 ft. (3 m)
Dense shrub has flattened clusters of creamy flowers that are succeeded by blue-black berries.

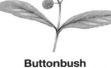

Buttonbush
Cephalanthus occidentalis
To 10 ft. (3 m)
"Pincushion" flowers have protruding stamens.

Fragrant Water Lily
Nymphaea odorata
Flower to 6 in.
(15 cm) wide.

Pussytoes
Antennaria spp.
To 16 in. (40 cm)
Woolly stalks support
fluffy flowerheads.

Bloodroot
Sanguinaria canadensis
To 10 in. (25 cm)
Root has a reddish
sap. One of the
earliest spring
flowers to bloom.

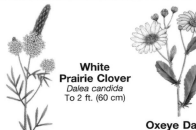

Dutchman's Breeches
Dicentra cucullaria
To 12 in. (30 cm)
Spurred flowers
resemble trousers.

Yarrow
Achillea millefolium
To 3 ft. (90 cm)
Leaves are
fern-like.

Fly Poison
Amianthium muscitoxicum
To 4 ft. (1.2 m)

Springcress
Cardamine bulbosa
To 2 ft. (60 cm)

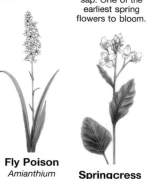

Jack-in-the-Pulpit
Arisaema triphyllum
To 3 ft. (90 cm)
Club-like stem is
surrounded by a
curving, green to
purplish hood.

Heath Aster
Aster ericoides
To 2 ft. (60 cm)

Queen Anne's Lace
Daucus carota
To 4 ft. (1.2 m)
Flower clusters become
cup-shaped as they age.

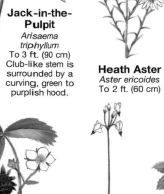

Wild Strawberry
Fragaria virginiana
Stems to 8 in. (20 cm)
Creeping plant has
5-petalled flowers
that are succeeded
by the familiar fruit.

Shooting Star
Dodecatheon spp.
To 20 in. (50 cm)
Flower petals are
white, rose or lilac.

Mayapple
Podophyllum peltatum
To 18 in. (45 cm)
Cup-shaped flowers
bloom between 2
leaves. Fruits are yellow.

White Prairie Clover
Dalea candida
To 2 ft. (60 cm)

Oxeye Daisy
Leucanthemum vulgare
To 3 ft. (90 cm)
Showy flowers bloom
along roadsides in summer.

Flowering Spurge
Euphorbia corollata
To 3 ft. (90 cm)

Bouncing Bet
Saponaria officinalis
To 3 ft. (90 cm)
Flowers are pinkish
to white.

White Larkspur
Delphinium carolinianum
To 3 ft. (90 cm)
Flowers are white
to blue.

Culver's Root
Veronicastrum virginicum
To 7 ft. (2.1 m)
Flowers are white to purplish.

Butterfly Weed
Asclepias tuberosa
To 3 ft. (90 cm)
Orange flowers
are star-shaped.

Tickseed
Coreopsis lanceolata
To 2 ft. (60 cm)
Note lance-shaped leaves
and notched flower rays.

Tickseed Sunflower
Bidens aristosa
To 5 ft. (1.5 m)

Partridge Pea
Cassia fasciculata
To 30 in. (75 cm)
Leaves have 6-18 pairs
of leaflets. Flowers have
brown centers.

Jewelweed
Impatiens capensis
To 5 ft. (1.5 m)
Spotted, orange-yellow
flowers are horn-shaped.
Ripe seed capsules
burst when touched.

Common Mullein
Verbascum thapsus
To 7 ft. (2.1 m)
Common
roadside weed.

Yellow Lady's Slipper
Cypripedium calceolus
To 28 in. (70 cm)

Sneezeweed
Helenium spp.
To 20 in. (50 cm)
Yellow flowers have a
dome-like central disk.

Yellow Jessamine
Gelsemium sempervirens
Vine to 17 ft. (5.1 m) long.

Common Sunflower
Helianthus annuus
To 9 ft. (2.7 m)
Flowers follow the sun
across the sky each day.

Common Evening Primrose
Oenothera spp.
To 5 ft. (1.5 m)
Lemon-scented,
4-petalled flowers
bloom in the evening.

Common St. John's Wort
Hypericum spp.
To 30 in. (75 cm)
Widespread weed is
found in waste areas.

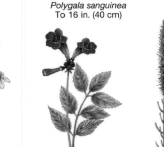

Yellow-fringed Orchid
Platanthera ciliaris
To 3 ft. (90 cm)

Gray-headed Coneflower
Ratibida pinnata
To 5 ft. (1.5 m)

Black-eyed Susan
Rudbeckia hirta
To 3 ft. (90 cm)
Flower has a dark,
conical central disk.

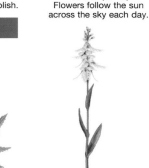

Hoary Puccoon
Lithospermum canescens
To 18 in. (45 cm)
Hairy plant has yellow-
orange tubular flowers.

Cup Plant
Silphium perfoliatum
To 8 ft. (2.4 m)

Goldenrod
Solidago spp.
To 5 ft. (1.5 m)
Flowers bloom in
arched clusters.

Field Milkwort
Polygala sanguinea
To 16 in. (40 cm)

Wild Ginger
Asarum canadense
To 12 in. (30 cm)
Flowers arise at base
of 2 leaves.

Columbine
Aquilegia canadensis
To 2 ft. (60 cm)

Trumpet Creeper
Campsis radicans
Vine to 20 ft. (6 m)

Prairie Blazing Star
Liatris pycnostachya
To 5 ft. (1.5 m)

Spotted Knapweed
Centaurea maculosa
To 4 ft. (1.2 m)
Dark-spotted near
flowerhead.

Fire Pink
Silene virginica
To 2 ft. (60 cm)

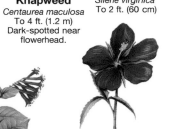

Small Red Morning Glory
Ipomoea coccinea
Vine to 9 ft. (2.7 m)

Trumpet Honeysuckle
Lonicera sempervirens
Vine to 17 ft. (5.1 m)

Rose Mallow
Hibiscus spp.
To 10 ft. (3 m)
Crimson flowers have
elongate styles.

Cardinal Flower
Lobelia cardinalis
To 4 ft. (1.2 m)

Teasel
Dipsacus sylvestris
To 7 ft. (2.1 m)

Phlox
Phlox longifolia
To 20 in. (50 cm)
Five-petalled, yellow-
centered flowers may
be white, yellow, pink,
red or lavender. Grows
in sprawling clusters.

Virginia Meadow Beauty
Rhexia virginica
To 2 ft. (60 cm)
Pink flowers have
8 yellow stamens.

Hedge Bindweed
Convolvulus sepium
Vine to 10 ft. (3 m)

Prairie Rose
Rosa arkansana
To 2 ft. (60 cm)

Indian Pink
Spigelia marilandica
To 2 ft. (60 cm)

Scarlet Paintbrush
Castilleja coccinea
To 2 ft. (60 cm)

Red Clover
Trifolium pratense
To 2 ft. (60 cm)
Leaves have 3 leaflets.

Chicory
Cichorium intybus
To 6 ft. (1.8 m)
Wheel-shaped
flowers are varying
shades of blue.

Purple Coneflower
Echinacea purpurea
To 5 ft. (1.5 m)

Closed Gentian
Gentiana andrewsii
To 2 ft. (60 cm)

Purple Prairie Clover
Dalea purpurea
To 3 ft. (90 cm)

Iris
Iris spp.
To 31 in.
(78 cm)

Vetch
Vicia spp.
Stems to 7 ft. (2.1 m)
Climbing vine has tubular,
pea-shaped flowers.

Aster
Aster spp.
To 12 in. (30 cm)

Wild Bergamot
Monarda fistulosa
To 4 ft. (1.2 m)

Passionflower
Passiflora incarnata
Climbing vine
to 20 ft. (6 m) high.
Flowers have a fringe
of "tentacles."

Violet Wood Sorrel
Oxalis violacea
To 6 in. (15 cm)

Blue-eyed Grass
Sisyrinchium angustifolium
To 2 ft. (60 cm)

Spiderwort
Tradescantia spp.
To 3 ft. (90 cm)

Common Morning Glory
Ipomoea purpurea
Stems to 10 ft. (3 m) long.
Creeping plant.

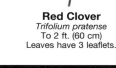

Venus' Looking Glass
Triodanis perfoliata
To 2 ft. (60 cm)
Note how leaves
"clasp" the stem.

Speedwell
Veronica spp.
To 8 in. (20 cm)
The bright blue flowers
have 4 petals with the
bottom one smallest.

Common Blue Violet
Viola papilionacea
To 8 in. (20 cm)

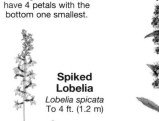

Birdfoot Violet
Viola pedata
To 10 in. (25 cm)
Leaves are
birdfoot-shaped.

Spiked Lobelia
Lobelia spicata
To 4 ft. (1.2 m)

Blueweed
Echium vulgare
To 30 in. (75 cm)
Blue flowers have
long, red stamens.
Also called viper's
bugloss. Invasive.